Exploring the Transfiguration Story

John Michael Perry

Sheed & Ward

Other titles in this series:
- *Exploring the Genesis Creation and Fall Stories*
- *Exploring the Resurrection of Jesus*
- *Exploring the Origins and Evolution of Eucharist in the New Testament*

Sheed & Ward™ is a service of The National Catholic Reporter Publishing Company.

Library of Congress Cataloguing-in-Publication Data

Perry, John M., 1929-
    Exploring the transfiguration story / John Michael Perry.
        p.   cm. -- (Exploring scripture series)
    ISBN 1-55612-574-7 (alk. paper)
    1. Jesus Christ--Transfiguration. 2. Bible. N.T. Mark IX,
2-8--Criticism, interpretation, etc. I. Title. II. Series: Perry,
John M., 1929-   Exploring scripture series.
BT410.P47 1993
232.9'56--dc20   92-26971
                                                                              CIP

Published by: Sheed & Ward
                 115 E. Armour Blvd.
                 P.O. Box 419492
                 Kansas City, MO 64141-6492

To order, call: (800) 333-7373

Contents

Part One: Introduction

AMONG THE STORIES IN THE SYNOPTIC GOSPELS (Mark, Matthew, and Luke) which narrate events that occurred during the public mission of Jesus, the strangest by far is the account of Jesus' Transfiguration. Since Mark's account was used by Matthew and Luke as the basis of their versions of this story, we will use Mark's account (9:2-8) for our considerations:

> And after six days Jesus took with him Peter and James and John, and led them up a high mountain apart by themselves; and he was transfigured before them. And his garments became glistening, intensely white, as no fuller on earth could bleach them. And there appeared to them Elijah with Moses; and they were talking to Jesus. And Peter said to Jesus, "Master, it is well that we are here; let us make three booths, one for you and one for Moses and one for Elijah." For he did not know what to say, for they were exceedingly afraid. And a cloud overshadowed them, and a voice came out of the cloud, "This is my beloved Son; listen to him." And suddenly looking around they no longer saw anyone with them but Jesus only (Mk 9:2-8).

There are, of course, a number of astonishing stories in the Gospels in which Jesus performs miraculous signs.

But all of these stories are related as taking place within the world of ordinary waking experience. The Transfiguration account, by contrast, stands out as not only astonishing, but even surreal. We suddenly realize that the mountain which Jesus has ascended in the company of Peter, James, and John has been transformed into the archetypal "mountain of revelation." (An archetype is a fundamental human experience widely and recurrently used to illustrate an invisible reality which it somehow resembles; e.g., the reality of a *high* mountain is used to symbolize "access" to the *higher* reality of the Sacred.)

Illustrious and long deceased prophets associated with the "mountain of revelation" have been summoned from the netherworld for a portentous conversation with the transfigured Jesus. Next, a mysterious cloud covers the mountain, and from the cloud God himself speaks to the awed disciples and informs them of the exalted Messianic dignity of Jesus. And then, just as suddenly as it began, the vision is over.

What should we make of such an amazing account? Should we understand it as an event which actually occurred during the public mission of Jesus, or should we read it as a symbolic story created by the early church to teach an important lesson about Jesus and his relation to Moses (the law) and Elijah (the prophets)? Contemporary biblical scholarship advises us to do the latter.

Vincent Taylor, in his commentary on Mark, has observed that in addition to the dreamlike quality of the Transfiguration story, it is difficult to see how the disciples could have asked the question about the coming of Elijah while coming down the mountain, (Mk. 9:11) or abandoned Jesus in fear and uncertainty in the Garden of Gethsemane (Mk. 14:50), if they had literally experienced the revelatory vision described in Mk 9:2-8.

The remainder of this monograph will be devoted to explaining that the Transfiguration account was created to teach an important *theological* lesson about Jesus and is not the memory of an actual historical event. In pursuit of this goal, we will examine the special historical circumstances that called the story into being. We will then ask ourselves why Mark decided to use the story in his Gospel and *placed* it where he did. Finally, we will consider a number of related questions that are usually prompted by the contemporary reading of the story.

From this point forward, readers are urged to open their Bibles and relate the explanation being provided to the indicated biblical text. This text will corroborate or clarify the matter being discussed. Readers who ignore this advice will fail to grasp much, if not most, of what is being explained.

Questions for Further Study

1. What are the features of the Transfiguration story that set it apart from the other stories about Jesus in the Gospels?

2. What is an archetype, and why should we expect to encounter archetypal symbols when reading the Bible?

3. Does modern biblical scholarship think we should read the Transfiguration story as literal history or as symbolic lesson about Jesus?

Part Two:
The Origin of the Account

1.

THE MAJOR CONFLICT which troubled the internal life of the early church was that which erupted over whether or not Gentile converts had to observe the entire law of Moses. The earliest Christians were Jewish Christians, and the most conservative among them insisted that the law of Moses and the writings of the prophets possessed authority fully equal to that of Jesus. They maintained, therefore, that Gentile converts to the Christian faith community were obliged to observe not only the moral precepts in the law of Moses, but all of the *purity* and *ceremonial* precepts as well (Acts 15:1-5).

Raymond E. Brown has suggested convincingly that at least three other groups of Jewish Christians differed with the most conservative Jewish Christians. These three dissenting groups allowed various degrees of *departure* from observance of Mosaic law. The *first* group did not require Gentile converts to receive circumcision or to observe Mosaic ceremonial laws. But it did require such converts to observe some purity laws involving food and sexual conduct so that coexistence with Jewish Christians in the same worshiping community would be facilitated

(Acts 15:14- 21,28-29; 21:25). We gather from the second chapter of Galatians that Peter, James, and Barnabas belonged to this group, and that its viewpoint prevailed at Antioch (see Acts 15:22- 34).

The *second* group also did not require circumcision or the observance of ceremonial laws. In addition, it did not require the observance of purity laws pertaining to food (1 Cor 10:27-29), although consideration for the scruples of others was strongly urged (1 Cor 8:1-13). This group did, however, require the observance of purity laws pertaining to sexual conduct (1 Cor 5:1- 2; 6:16-18). And while it did not require observance of ceremonial law, it did allow (in common with the first group above) that Jewish Christians might find devotional value in such practices (Acts 18:18; 21:23-24). Paul was probably the best known spokesman for the second group in the apostolic church.

The *third* group not only denied the need to observe Mosaic ceremonial and dietary precepts, but was even *hostile* toward such observance and its related Jewish institutions. This position was represented by the antitemple stance of Stephen in the early church (Acts 6-7) and by the Fourth Evangelist near the turn of the first century (John 4:20-24).

As we proceed it will become evident that the Transfiguration story was called into being by the bitter disagreement between ultraconservative Jewish Christians and the *moderating* Jewish Christians in the early church. The story was probably created by an inspired teacher from the *first* group of moderates as his church's *midrashic* answer to the pressing question of Mosaic observance. The reasons for placing this teacher within the first group, possibly at Antioch, will be given below.

2.

BEFORE WE PROCEED WITH OUR TASK, we should spend some time clarifying the term *midrash* which was used in its adjectival form just above. Midrash was a method created by the ancient Jewish scribes (biblical scholars) for finding contemporary meaning in the ancient Jewish scriptures. Midrashic teaching could be either oral or written, and could take the form of *halakah* (interpretations of law) or *haggadah* (religious lessons that were nonlegal in nature).

At some time during the postexilic period (after 538 B.C.) the scribes began teaching the Jews that everything God intended to do in history was already foreshadowed in the law of Moses and in the writings of the prophets. Therefore, only those interpretations of law and religious belief which could be shown to have a midrashic basis in scripture were acceptable.

Accordingly, the scribes searched the scriptures for texts that seemed to portend and corroborate their interpretations of present problems or anticipated developments. They would then either quote the ancient text chosen to validate their teaching, or they would allude to it by weaving one or more of its key words into their presentation. Either way, the confirming text was always indicated in a manner recognizable by those familiar with the scriptures and the midrashic method of teaching.

The importance of midrash in the religious life of ancient Judaism was greatly increased after Hellenistic Syria began to cruelly persecute the Jews for their monotheism in 168 B.C. In addition to provoking the Maccabean Revolt in 165 B.C. (see 1 Macc 1:1-2:68), the Syrian persecution caused a major religious crisis for devout Jews. This crisis was resolved with the help of midrash.

Traditional Jewish theology had long assumed that those who faithfully served God would be rewarded unfailingly by a long and happy life *in this world.* (Blessing from God was expected during one's life on earth, after which one would have to go to sheol, the place of the dead, as punishment for Adam's sin.) During the Syrian persecution, however, it became painfully evident that this belief was being contradicted. Large numbers of Jews who were determined to serve the one true God were executed. Apostates, conversely, were spared and even rewarded. An anonymous Jewish teacher was inspired by God to resolve the resulting faith crisis by the creation of "apocalyptic" theology.

Apocalyptic theology made its debut in the book of Daniel in 165 B.C. This important book introduced "eschatological" hope to faithful Jews during the religious crisis caused by the Syrian persecution. Eschatology teaches that the world will someday end (Dan 12:4,13). On that day the dead will be raised and judged along with the living (Dan 12:2). After the final judgment, the righteous will enjoy unending life in the New Creation (Dan 12:3). The wicked, however, will receive everlasting punishment in return for their deeds (Dan 12:2). Until the book of Daniel was written, the ancient Jews did not believe in the possibility of unending life and joy beyond death.

The book of Daniel justified its *novel* eschatological teaching by means of midrash (e.g., Dan 2:34-35,44-45 is based on Is 28:16; 2:2. Dan 7:6,12-14 is based on Gen 1:26; Ps 8:3-6. Dan 9:24-27 is based on Jer 29:10-11 [see Dan 9:2]. Dan 12:1b is based on Is 33:2. Dan 12:1c is based on Ex 32:32-33; Dan 12:2 is based on Ps 3:5. Dan 12:3 is based on Gen 15:5; 22:17. Dan 12:4a is based on Zeph 1:18). The eschatological hope introduced in the book of Daniel was *fully embraced* by the Pharisees but was *never accepted* by the Sadduccees (see Mk 12:18 and Acts 23:6-8).

During the period in the early church when the Gospels were being written, midrash had become the prevailing theological method among Palestinian Jews for teaching about God's purpose in history. We should bear in mind that the first Christians were Jews who had learned about midrash in the synagogue. These Jewish Christians carried out the major part of their witnessing to the Jews while attending the synagogue (Acts 6:9; 13:13-43). It was inevitable, therefore, that they would appeal to the authority of midrash in order to advance and defend their claims about the Messiahship of Jesus.

For the Jewish Christians who constituted the earliest church, it was the Risen Jesus who had conclusively fulfilled all of the "promises" of salvation found in the scriptures. These Jewish Christians were utterly convinced that Jesus and his unexpected Messianic destiny were mysteriously foreshadowed in the law and the prophets. We should not be surprised to learn, then, that the Gospels are filled with midrashic teaching about Jesus. Sometimes this teaching takes the form of explicit *quotations* (e.g., Matt. 1:22-23; 2:5-6; Jn 19:24,37), but more frequently midrashic *allusions* are woven into the stories being narrated to avoid interrupting them (e.g., Luke 1:26-27, 32-33; Mk 14:20; 15:24).

On occasion, two or three foreshadowing proof texts are combined into one citation in the New Testament. For example, the quotation attributed to Isaiah in Mark 1:2-3 is actually a midrashic conflation of Mal 3:1; Ex 23:20; and Is 40:3. All of these texts were thought by Mark to foreshadow the mission of John the Baptizer as prophetic precursor of Jesus. Unless we are well versed in the scriptures and informed about midrash, we will frequently fail to grasp what the Gospels truly intend to teach about Jesus. We also will fall into historical and theological error by taking *nonliteral* statements literally.

Theologizing in the midrashic mode may strike us as strange. Nevertheless, to the earliest Christians it seemed to be the only means to successfully bring their faith claims about Jesus to the Jews, especially when witnessing in the synagogue. If we make the effort to understand the viewpoint of Jewish-Christian midrash, we will discover that it is filled with theological meaning and beauty, and is often (as we will see in the case of the Transfiguration story) the key that unlocks the authentic meaning of the Gospels.

3.

CENTRAL TO THE QUESTION of Mosaic observance were the respective authorities of *Moses* and *Jesus*. Although the adherents of the "circumcision party" (Acts 11:2) maintained that the authority of Moses was equal to that of Jesus (Acts 15:1,5), the moderating Jewish Christians disagreed (Acts 15:6-29). The moderates venerated the law of Moses as the word of God, but believed that the law had been destined from its outset to be brought to perfection by Jesus, who is its fulfillment (Matt 5:17-19; Gal 3:24-25; Jn 5:46).

To validate their conviction, the moderates searched the scriptures for midrashic proof texts which would verify that the teaching authority of Jesus was destined to eclipse that of Moses (and the other prophets). They found the most important of such texts in Deut 18:15 where Moses himself is described as delivering the following oracle:

> The Lord your God will raise up for you
> a prophet like me from among you, from
> your brethren—him you shall heed.

Modern scholarship knows that in its original intent this passage did not literally promise a New Moses destined to supersede Moses of old. Rather, it promised that God would raise up a prophet from time to time to instruct Israel as Moses had done.

The moderating Jewish Christians in the early church, however, could not have approached this text in such an objective and scientific fashion. They brought to it their historically conditioned beliefs about *midrash* and concluded that the reference to a prophet like Moses to be "raised up" in the future portended that Jesus would be Resurrected as the New Moses, endowed with glory and authority far greater than that of the old Moses (Acts 3:22-26; 7:37). They justified this conclusion with the following interpretation: When Moses of old came down from the "mountain of revelation" with the tables of God's law, his face (but *only* his face) was transformed with such radiance that he had to wear a veil among the frightened Israelites until the glory eventually faded (Ex 34:29-35).

(A critical modern reader will notice that Ex 34:29-35 does not state that the radiance shining from Moses' face eventually faded. But at the time of the early church no one read scripture "critically," and it was assumed that since the radiance is not mentioned in later stories about Moses, it must have faded.)

On the other hand, the Risen Jesus was experienced by his disciples as *totally* transfigured by God with the *permanent* glory of Everlasting Life. The moderating Jewish Christians in the early church understood this contrast as a midrashic sign from God that the authority of Moses was destined to be temporary, whereas that of the Risen Jesus, the New Moses, was revealed as definitive and unending.

In 2 Cor 3:7-13,18 Paul explicitly makes this midrashic comparison (Had he learned it during his stay at Antioch?):

Now if the dispensation of death, carved in letters on stone, came with such splendor that the Israelites could not look at Moses' face because of its brightness, fading as it was, will not the dispensation of the Spirit be attended with greater splendor? . . . Indeed, in this case, what once had splendor has come to have no splendor at all, because of the splendor that surpasses it. For if what faded away came with splendor, what is permanent must have much more splendor . . . not like Moses who put a veil over his face so that the Israelites might not see the end of the fading splendor. . . . And we all, with unveiled face, beholding the glory of the Lord, are being changed into his likeness from one degree of glory to another.

The Gospel of Matthew suggests the same comparison between the passing authority of Moses of old (5:21, 31, 33, 38, 43) and the permanent authority of Jesus, the New Moses (28:18, 20). Matthew has Jesus begin his prophetic mission on the archetypal "mountain of revelation" (5:1-2; 8:1) to evoke the memory of Moses at Sinai. The *culminating* revelatory appearance of the Risen Jesus is located by Matthew on the same archetypal "mountain" to remind us that Jesus has been "raised up" as the "prophet like" Moses (28:16).

The Fourth Evangelist also indicates midrashically that Jesus is "the prophet" like Moses (Jn 6:14). For we read in the Fourth Gospel that Jesus, the New Moses, after going up on the "mountain of revelation" at Passover time (6:3-4), feeds the multitude which has followed him with *true* manna (6:32), far superior to that provided by Moses of old (6:35-50).

In like manner, some moderating Jewish Christian in the early church created the Transfiguration story to teach that the authority of Jesus was destined to surpass that of Moses. To provide an appropriate context for his midrashic comparison of Jesus and Moses, this teacher depicted Jesus going up on the mountain of revelation "after six days" to communicate with God on the seventh day (Mk 9:2) just as *Moses* did in Ex 24:15-16:

> Then Moses went up on the mountain and a cloud covered the mountain. The glory of the Lord settled on Mount Sinai, and covered it six days; and on the seventh day he called to Moses out of the midst of the cloud.

We are told by the moderating teacher that when Jesus goes up the mountain he is accompanied by Peter, James, and John (Mk 9:2), who were remembered by the gospel tradition as privileged witnesses to esoteric revelatory events (Mk 5:37; 1 Cor 15:5; Lk 24:34; Jn 21:1-2). While they are with Jesus on the mountain, he is radiantly transfigured before them in a manner which reminds us of the permanent glory of his Resurrection to Everlasting Life. They also see Moses, who represents the *law*, and Elijah, the *prophets*, appearing and speaking with Jesus (Mk 9:4. The basis for identifying Moses with the law and Elijah with the prophets will be provided below in the answer to question 3 of Part Four). Significantly, we are not told that Moses and Elijah are radiantly transfigured, but *only* Jesus.

Peter then declares with astonishment that it is good that he and the other disciples are there to witness such an awe-inspiring convocation of God's prophets (Mk 9:5). He goes on to suggest that he and the other disciples should build *three* tabernacles (skēnas; the same word is found in Ex 25:8-9; 40:34-35 in the *Septuagint*, i.e., the Greek translation of the Hebrew scriptures used by Greek-speaking Jews after 250 B.C. Midrashic references to the Old Testament found in the Greek New Testament are usually taken from the Septuagint, which became the Bible of Greek-speaking Christians.)

The first of the three tabernacles recommemded by Peter is meant to signify and honor God's revealing presence in Jesus, the second and third are meant to do the same respectively for Moses and Elijah. *Equal* honor and authority, therefore, are imputed to all three prophets—which alludes to the position of the ultraconservative Jewish Christians. Peter is apparently so overawed by this gathering of prophetic notables that he fails to understand why Jesus has been singled out *exclusively* for transfiguration.

When we reach Mk 9:6, an editorial voice intervenes and implies that there is something obtuse and unseemly about Peter's suggestion (ou gar ēdei ti apokrithē, "for he did not know what he was saying"). We will see below (in the answer to question 5 of Part Four) that there are good reasons for thinking that this verse, which calls attention to the spiritual blindness of Peter and the other disciples, was added to the original account by Mark. If it is omitted, the story flows with greater internal consistency.

Peter's suggestion in Mk 9:5 indicates that he has failed to grasp why Jesus has been singled out for transfiguration. Such preferment signifies the preeminence of Jesus over Moses and the other prophets, whose role it was to *prepare* for Jesus. We should assume that during their appearance Moses and Elijah are discussing with Jesus the scriptural adumbrations of God's purpose which Jesus is about to fulfill. (The Greek of Luke 9:30-31 tells us that Moses and Elijah were speaking with Jesus about his coming "exodon" [*exodus* or departure], "which he was to accomplish at Jerusalem.")

Peter has also failed to realize that the revealing presence of God is "tabernacling" (i.e., indwelling as in a movable sanctuary) definitively in Jesus. (The Greek of the midrash in Jn 1:14 actually says that the Word became flesh and "tabernacled" among us.) Consequently, the "cloud" which is described in the book of Exodus as covering the "tabernacle" of old (Ex 40:34-35) now covers the transfigured Jesus while he is conversing with Moses and

Elijah. Moses of old was remembered as having *entered* the tabernacle (Ex 33:7-10). Jesus, on the other hand, has *become* the tabernacle.

God then speaks from the cloud (as he is described in the the book of Exodus as having spoken to Moses) and admonishes Peter and the other two disciples to recognize that Jesus is the Messianic Son of God (Ps 2:7; see 2 Sam 7:12-14) and also the prophet like Moses, whom God has "raised up" (Deut 18:15) to unending glory. (The midrashic logic of the Transfiguration account presupposes that the Resurrection of Jesus has already been revealed to the Christian faith community.)

Furthermore, since it is (the Risen) Jesus who now "enshrines" the revealing presence of God permanently and incomparably, Peter and the other disciples should "listen to him" as the one endowed with definitive authority and should not assign *equal* authority to Moses and the prophets. The words that God speaks when he commands Peter to listen to Jesus (akouete autou, "listen to him"), are almost identical to the words that God is described as speaking through Moses in the Greek version of Deut 18:15 when directing Israel to "listen" to the prophet "like" Moses (autou akousesthe, "him you shall listen to"). Only the verb tenses differ.

4.

IT WAS SUGGESTED EARLIER that the creator of the Transfiguration account probably belonged to the *first* of the various groups of Jewish Christians who favored mitigation of the law, and that he possibly wrote at Antioch. This conclusion is based on the following indications:

(1) Peter seems to have been known in the Apostolic church as the chief spokesman for the moderating Jewish Christians of the *first* type. (That is why he is singled out

for special honor and given singular authority in Matthew's Gospel 16:17-19; 17:24-27, which was probably written at Antioch). It is significant that Peter is also the spokesman for the disciples in the Transfiguration account. (2) Antioch probably became the center for Jewish Christians of the *first* persuasion, and Peter himself resided there for a time (Gal 2:11-14). (3) Peter (the Rock, Matt 16:18) was celebrated in the early church as the first witness to the appearances of the Risen Jesus (1 Cor 15:5; Luke 24:34). In the Transfiguration account he is described as receiving a revelation from God that makes *explicit* the peerless authority of Jesus already *implicit* in the Resurrection appearances. (4) Even though Moses and Elijah are subordinated to Jesus in the Transfiguration account, they nevertheless are treated as deserving of great honor and are closely associated with Jesus. This view accords with the greater measure of respect for the law which characterized the least extreme of the moderating Jewish Christians whose center seems to have been at Antioch.

One might object that since Peter is reprimanded in the account for assigning too much authority to Moses and the prophets, the moderating position which he historically represented with respect to the law is being rejected. That reading is possible but seems unlikely for two reasons: (1) The theological stance seemingly advocated by Peter in the Transfiguration account is contrary to the moderating position which he is known to have embraced historically. (2) It is far more likely that Peter's celebrity as the first Resurrection witness is being cleverly employed to lend authority to the moderating position being advanced by the account. Peter is presented by the account as having received divine reprimand *and* instruction concerning the account's theological position. And if the ultraconservatives objected that they knew of no such tradition, the reputation of Peter, James, and John as privileged witnesses to esoteric revelatory events (Mk 5:37; 1 Cor 15:5; Lk 24:34; Jn 21:2-12) could be appealed to.

Questions for Further Study

1. What was the most serious problem that disrupted the internal life of the early church?

2. What is midrash? When and why was midrash created?

3. Why is an understanding of midrash important for anyone who hopes to grasp the authentic meaning of the Gospels?

4. What is a proof text, and why should we expect to find proof texts in the Gospels?

5. What has the person who created the Transfiguration story revealed to us about his or her theological views?

Part Three:
Mark's Use of the Account

1.

THE TRANSFIGURATION STORY WAS ALREADY KNOWN to Mark when he began writing his Gospel. He decided to include the story as an important part of the *Messianic Secret theology* which he created and strategically located throughout his Gospel. The hidden and unexpected nature of Jesus' Messiahship is the overarching concern of Mark's Gospel from beginning to end.

Mark was preoccupied with Messianic Secret theology because he believed it provided the correct answer for two important questions still being wrestled with by his church. The first question had been addressed to Christians during the course of their debates with the Jews. The second question was being asked by members of the Christian faith community and is closely related to the first. We will consider these questions in turn.

The more pressing of the two questions which concerned Mark and his church had been raised by the insistence of the Jews that Jesus was *not* the kind of Messiah their tradition had taught them to expect. How could Jesus be the Messiah promised to Israel, the Jews demanded, if the majority of the Jews and their religious leaders refused to acknowledge him as such? Answering this question was the most urgent theological task confronting the early Christians.

The earliest Christians were Jewish Christians; they believed that God's plan of salvation for Israel and the nations was presaged in the scriptures. Consequently, they searched the scriptures for midrashic proof texts which would vindicate their faith in a Messiah unexpectedly rejected by the very people to whom he had been sent. They soon found several texts which they believed foreshadowed Jesus' rejection by the "chief priests" of the Jews and by the "majority" of the Jewish people. The most important of these texts was Ps 118:22-23.

> The stone which the builders rejected has become
> the head of the corner. This is the Lord's doing; it
> is marvelous in our eyes.

We can tell that this passage was extremely important in the "apologetic" theology of the earliest church; it is the Old Testament text most frequently quoted (Mk 12:10; Mt 21:42; Lk 20:17; Acts 4:11; 1 Pet 2:7) or alluded to (Mark 8:31; Luke 7:30; 9:22; 17:25; 1 Pet 2:4,7) in the New Testament. (Apologetics is teaching designed to defend religious beliefs from attack.)

When the ancient author of Ps 118 spoke of "builders" in vs. 22, he was probably referring figuratively to the enemies of Israel and her kings (the persons speaking and spoken of in this psalm are difficult to identify). But to Jewish Christians searching for midrashic proof texts, the "builders" were judged to be the Jewish leaders who, by rejecting Jesus, had unwittingly fulfilled God's secret purpose foreintended in his word (see Jn 11:49-51).

Another important text which the early Christians thought foreshadowed Jesus' rejection is Is 6:9-10:

> Go and say to this people: 'Hear and hear, but do
> not understand; see and see, but do not perceive.

> Make the heart of this people fat, and their ears
> heavy, and shut their eyes; lest they see with their
> eyes, and hear with their ears, and understand
> with their hearts, and turn and be healed.'

When the prophet Isaiah delivered this oracle, he was not speaking of the way in which, centuries later, the majority of the Jews would reject Christian claims about the Messiahship of Jesus. Instead, Isaiah was chiding the Israelites of his own day for their lack of faith in the words God had spoken to them through the prophets. But, again, to the earliest Christians, Is 6:9-10 seemed to foretell the rejection of Jesus by the majority of his people. This passage is either quoted or alluded to in all four Gospels and in the Acts of the Apostles (Mk 4:2; Mt 13:14-15; Lk 8:10; John 12:40; Acts 28:27).

When we consider the frequent citation of Is 6:9-10, the even more frequent references to Ps 118:22-23, and Paul's brooding reflection in Romans 9-11 on the riddle of Israel's refusal, we realize that the rejection of Jesus by the Jewish majority was a problem of the first magnitude for the apostolic church. Mark is providing a solution for this problem with his Messianic Secret theology, and he uses the two texts just cited as important parts of that theology. (See Mk 4:11-12 and 12:10-11.)

2.

THE SECOND AND CLOSELY RELATED QUESTION about the Messiahship of Jesus was raised by Jesus' unusual response to the title "Messiah" on several occasions during his public ministry. The first of these occasions took place at Caesarea Philippi (Mk 8:27) when Jesus asked his disciples privately who they thought he was (Mk 8:29). Peter replied, "You are the Messiah."

The majority of contemporary biblical scholars think that Jesus' original response to Peter's assertion in Mk 8:29 is preserved not in 8:30-31, but in 8:33. If we move directly from 8:29 to 8:33, we are led to conclude that Jesus rejected Peter's attribution of Messiahship and rebuked Peter harshly saying, "Get behind me Satan! For you are not on the side of God, but of men." (See the role of Satan in Mt 4:8-10 and Lk 4:5-7.)

This interpretation seems probable to the majority for two reasons: (1) Jesus clearly preferred the title "Son of Man" (found on his lips 67 times in the Gospels, including parallels) and avoided the title "Messiah" (found on his lips only in Mk 12:35, and its parallels in Matthew and Luke). Moreover, this passage is judged by most scholars to be a theological creation of the early church. It is used by Mark to suggest that there is something mysterious about the promised Messiah that will defy traditional expectations. (2) The teaching in Mk 8:30-31 about the hidden and unexpected nature of Jesus' Messiahship has the characteristics of Mark's Messianic Secret theology (which will be explained below). Since Mark joined elements of this theology to a number of other stories in his Gospel, these elements are easily detected and compared. (It is not the purpose of this monograph to present a thorough discussion of the Messianic Secret motif in Mark's Gospel; only those ideas necessary for understanding his use of the Transfiguration story will be examined.)

Mark and others in the early church were engaged by the memory that Jesus had responded so *disapprovingly* when Peter confessed his belief in Jesus' Messiahship. They were convinced that the prophetic promises of a Davidic Messiah had to be fulfilled, and they believed that Jesus was descended from King David (Rom 1:3; Mt 1:1-17; Lk 3:23-38). They concluded, therefore, that God had revealed the Risen Jesus to them as the promised Davidic Messiah (Acts 2:32-33). Why, then, had Jesus refused to either accept (Mk 8:33) or discuss (Mk 15:2-5) the title Messiah?

Mark realized, of course, that Jesus had turned out to be a completely unexpected kind of Messiah, a *spiritual* Messiah, not the invincible *military* Messiah of popular expectation. But Mark assumed that Jesus, since he is the greatest of God's prophets, had been secretly informed by God of the hidden nature of his Messiahship at the beginning of his mission.

For this reason, Mark relates that God revealed the Messianic Secret to Jesus on the occasion of his Baptism-anointing (1:9-11) by John the priest-prophet. (John was the son of Zechariah the priest, therefore, a priest as well as a prophet.) By describing Jesus as secretly anointed by the Spirit (1:10) through the mediation of John, Mark is also midrashically solving another problem. If Jesus is truly David's greatest son and Israel's promised Messiah, he should have have been "anointed" as such, ideally by a priest and prophet (see 1 Kgs 1:32-34, 38-39). We are assured by Mark that Jesus was anointed by one who was both priest *and* prophet, John the son of Zechariah. But Jesus was not anointed in the ordinary manner with consecrated oil that symbolized the conferring of God's Spirit. Jesus was directly anointed by the very Spirit of God.

Mark assumed, therefore, that Jesus had been secretly anointed as a *spiritual* Messiah and that Jesus knew he was destined in God's hidden purpose to undergo tragic rejection and death (like the mysterious Suffering Servant of God in Is 52:13-53:12; see Mark 10:45). In addition, Mark thought Jesus knew that after his death, he would be raised as the exalted Son of Adam alluded to in Dan 7:13-14 and would soon return as God's glorious Son of Man-Messiah at the end of history (Mk 14:62). (The word for "man" in Hebrew is "adam." The eschatological title "Son of Man," then, really means "Son of Adam.")

(Some scholars object that the "Son of Man" spoken of in Dan 7:13-14 is not an individual but an eschatological figure who represents the Jewish people collectively. But even if that oversimplified opinion were true, it would not have been evident to the Christians in the earliest church who read scripture precritically and midrashed "atomistically," i.e., they ignored the *context* in which they found an appropriate midrashic text.)

It was Mark's judgment, accordingly, that Jesus had responded harshly to Peter at Caesarea Philippi because Jesus knew that Peter expected him to be the Messiah of *popular* expectation rather than the Messiah mysteriously destined for rejection and crucifixion before his exaltation. Jesus must have understood, Mark concluded, that his disciples would not be able to grasp the true nature of his Messiahship until that Secret was *fully* disclosed by the spiritual victory of his Resurrection. (See Mark 9:9-10.) It was for this reason, therefore, that Jesus avoided the title Messiah during his public mission.

In effect, Mark and other teachers before him in the early church were compelled by the tragic and unexpected developments in the history of Jesus to *redefine* the title Messiah and make it compatible with that history. Only in this fashion could the title be retained and assigned to the Risen Jesus, to whom they knew it mysteriously belonged. Mark then surmised that the new meaning which he and others had assigned to the title Messiah was present in the mind of Jesus throughout Jesus' public mission. Understandably, this "redefining" of the title Messiah by Christians led to fierce disagreements with the Jews.

Not only Jews, but even some who considered themselves to be faithful disciples of Jesus were unwilling to confess him as "Messiah." These disciples remembered (or had been told) that Jesus had reacted negatively to the title Messiah on several occasions. They concluded, therefore, that the title should not be assigned to him. They preferred to designate Jesus as the "Son of Man" (the earliest of the confessional titles conferred on the Risen Jesus; see Acts 7:56). Jesus was remembered by these disciples as having preferred that title when speaking of the eschatological king who would come to inaugurate the reign of God (Lk 12:8; Mk 8:38).

It is probably for this reason that Jesus is *never* given the title Messiah in the "Q sayings." (The Q sayings are an early collection of sayings attributed to Jesus. They were put in written form c. 55 A.D. and were included by Matthew and Luke in their Gospels.) It seems fair to conclude that the author of these sayings did not think the title Messiah was appropriate for Jesus.

This suggests that Mark created his Messianic Secret theology not only to equip his community for debate with the Jews, but also to answer the objections of those followers of Jesus (no doubt, a minority) who were unwilling to give Jesus the title Messiah. Mark's theological disagreement with these dissenting disciples is possibly the reason why he did not include the Q sayings in his Gospel (as did Matthew and Luke). He obviously would not have wished to lend authority to the non-Messianic viewpoint of the Q sayings by including them in his sacred history of Jesus.

The ideas reviewed above should help us see that the teaching of Jesus in Mk 8:30-31 about the secret (8:30) and unexpected (8:31) nature of his Messiahship was added to the original story by Mark. These verses are Mark's *interpretation* of Jesus' negative response to Peter: Jesus did not totally reject the title "Messiah," but had grave reservations about the title because of the mistaken military expectations associated with it. Mark sincerely believed that the ideas he attributed to Jesus in 8:30-31 were the ideas that motivated Jesus when he rebuked Peter.

Contemporary scholarship would say that Mark's Messianic Secret theology contains a fundamental insight that is correct and important for Christian faith, but it also contains an assumption which is historically conditioned and mistaken. His *correct insight* is that God truly had destined Jesus for a mysterious and exalted Messiahship which was contrary to popular expectation, and would only be understood after Jesus' death and Resurrection.

Mark's *mistaken assumption* is that Jesus, because he is God's definitive eschatological prophet, knew all about God's secret Messianic purpose for him from the time of his Baptism. In actuality, the only one who understood the Messianic Secret throughout Jesus' public ministry was *God*.

Because of Jesus' radical commitment to the will of God, Jesus was certainly open throughout his prophetic ministry to whatever additional office God would eventually call him. The evidence indicates, however, that God did not reveal the Messianic Secret to Jesus till the time of Jesus' Resurrection. (The reason why Jesus' Messiahship was destined to be hidden will be discussed below in the answer to question 12 of Part Four.)

Some people are understandably upset when they learn that Jesus did not know he was God's Messiah before his Resurrection. If we find ourselves among their number, we should ask ourselves (with encouragement from William James) what difference it truly makes if Jesus did not learn about his Messianic office until *after* he had faithfully fulfilled its unexpected requirements. Does this make him less acceptable as the revelatory sign through whom God assures us of Eternal Life? On the contrary, it is easier to identify with Jesus as a divinely provided example of faith and trust in God if we assume that he did not have certainty about the future events in his life and their glorious outcome.

Mark, of course, should not be faulted for having unwittingly woven mistaken assumptions into his sacred history of Jesus. We may safely infer that Mark honestly did the best job he was capable of in God's service. As for God's view of this matter, God knew that the future, with its eventual increase in knowledge, would teach us to winnow Mark's mistaken assumptions from his correct insights.

3.

TWO OTHER OCCASIONS when Jesus responded perplexingly to the title "Messiah" were his separate interrogations by the Jewish high priest and the Roman procurator. It will be more convenient if we reverse the order found in the Gospels and begin with the questioning of Jesus by the Roman procurator, Pontius Pilate.

All of the Gospels report that when Pilate asked Jesus if he was the "king" of the Jews, Jesus responded laconically by reminding Pilate that it was Pilate, and not Jesus, who had invoked that title (Mk 15:2; Mt 27:11; Lk 23:3; Jn 18:37). The words of Jesus' response to Pilate (su legeis, "The words are yours [not mine]") are exactly the same in all four Gospels. These words are easily overlooked in the Fourth Gospel's theologically expanded dialog between Jesus and Pilate, but are still detectable.

In effect, Jesus refused to discuss the title Messiah (king was the Roman equivalent of Messiah), probably because he considered it theologically bankrupt and in no way related to his prophetic mission. To Pilate, however, Jesus' noncommital response probably seemed ominous, and it was possibly this which sealed Jesus' fate. Since Jesus would not *explicitly* deny that he was the "king" of the Jews, Pilate probably suspected him of harboring Messianic ambition and decided that Jesus would have to be executed as a potential threat to Rome. This interpretation is supported by the sign Pilate placed on the cross of Jesus to notify and warn the public of Jesus' crime: "Jesus of Nazareth, king of the Jews."

Mark relates that before Jesus was questioned by Pilate, he was questioned by the Jewish high priest at what purports to have been a formal trial. A number of scholars think, however, that the early church did not have precise information about the private interrogation of Jesus by the high priest. To compensate for this gap in her knowledge, the church would have *inferred* what must have taken place on the basis of Jesus' trial before Pilate. (The church probably did have some information about the Roman trial.) It is noteworthy that in the Fourth Gospel, which sometimes provides more accurate information about the passion history, Jesus is interrogated by Annas before he is sent to Caiaphas (Jn 18:19-24), and there is no suggestion of a formal Jewish "trial."

Be that as it may, it is highly probable that Jesus was at least questioned by the Jewish authorities. The Fourth Gospel does not tell us whether the high priest asked Jesus if he was the Messiah; the other three Gospels, however, relate that he *did* ask Jesus that question. Matthew (26:64) and Luke (22:70) agree (contrary to Mark) that Jesus' reply was essentially the same as the noncommital answer he was known to have given to Pilate.

Only Mark tells us in 14:62 that Jesus answered the high priest's question affirmatively (ego eimi, "I am"). But since Jesus is remembered as having given the *noncommital* response six out of seven times in the Gospels (four times to Pilate, two times to Jewish authorities) it seems likely that the one time he is presented as answering affirmatively is *not* history. Instead, it is Mark's theological *interpretation* of Jesus' noncommital reply.

The Messianic Secret theology which led Mark to "interpret" Jesus' puzzling response to Peter at Caesarea

Philippi also led Mark to "interpret" the response Jesus was remembered (or assumed) to have made to the high priest. Mark thought that the remembered unwillingness of Jesus to discuss the title Messiah (or king) was a sign of Jesus' prophetic certainty that his interrogators were incapable of understanding that title's "secret" meaning.

Jesus' decision to accept his tragic death was understood by Mark as the *beginning* of the process which Jesus knew would lead to his exaltation and the full disclosure of the Messianic Secret. Given that presupposition, it seemed theologically fitting to Mark to present Jesus as *beginning* to reveal the Secret publicly by a "Messianic" response to the high priest.

The affirmative response made by Jesus to the high priest, therefore, is followed by a majestic allusion to Jesus' imminent exaltation and expected return as the Son of Man (14:62). Explicit reference to the Servant theme, however, is prudently avoided by Jesus lest the powers of darkness discern the "Secret" prematurely and reverse the process that will lead to his death and exaltation.

Mark thought that his *theological* reading of Jesus' laconic response was fully justified by midrashic portendings in God's word and by the Resurrection of Jesus. It was assumed by Mark that his interpretation merely indicated midrashically what Jesus must have been thinking when he gave his noncommital answer. This method of narrating Jesus' response enabled Mark to simultaneously recount *and* explain Jesus' enigmatic behavior.

Messianic Secret theology, then, was intended by Mark to equip his church with the answers necessary for defending their faith in Jesus' Messiahship. This defense, Mark realized, had to be maintained on two fronts, for it was not only the Jews who refused to acknowledge Jesus as Messiah. We saw above that some of Jesus' disciples were also unwilling to give him that problematic title. It is likely that Mark was just as eager to convince the second group as the first.

4.

NOW THAT WE HAVE GAINED SOME INSIGHT into the reasons why Mark created his Messianic Secret theology, we are in a better position to understand the role which he intended the Transfiguration story to play in his Gospel. We saw above that Mark thought God must have revealed the Secret to Jesus on the occasion of his Baptism-anointing in the Jordan. Along with the early church, Mark was convinced that the midrashic foreshadowings of God's hidden Messianic purpose could be gathered and assembled like the pieces of a puzzle. The assembled pieces would then reveal or confirm the mysterious Messianic destiny of Jesus.

Accordingly, on the occasion of Jesus' Baptism, Mark has God address Jesus with the words, "You are my beloved Son, with you I am well pleased" (1:11). These words are a midrashic *combination* of Ps 2:7, Gen 22:2, and Is 42:1 (see Mt 12:18). They are meant, along with other symbols in the account, to signify that Jesus is being secretly informed that he is God's Servant-Messiah (Servant: Is 42:1; Messiah: Ps 2:7). As God's Servant-Messiah, he is destined to suffer an atoning death as the true Isaac (Gen 22:2). But after his death he will be vindicated as the exalted Son of Man (Dan 7:13-14) or New Adam who leads God's children into the New Creation. (The reason for positing an allusion to the apocalyptic Son of Man will follow below.)

In addition to the words spoken by God at the Baptism, Mark's mention of the anointing "Spirit" descending upon Jesus as a "dove" is also part of the revelation of the Messianic Secret to Jesus. Mark intends us to recall the

"Spirit" bestowed on God's Servant in Is 42:1 and the "dove" in Gen 8:10-11 that brings an olive leaf to Noah as a sign that the cleansing floodwaters of God's wrath have subsided and creation can begin anew.

Since Noah was a second Adam, he was viewed by the early church as a midrashic foreshadowing of Jesus, the New Adam, who gives us the new life of the Spirit through the new birth of Baptism. And since the old creation began with the Spirit of God moving over the primordial waters (Gen 1:2), it was midrashically fitting to describe the same Spirit as descending on Jesus, the New Adam, at his Baptism-anointing in the waters of the Jordan.

The eschatological king alluded to as "one like a son of man" in Daniel 7:13-14 is inseparably bound up with the New Adam theme in Mark's account of Jesus' Baptism. To fully grasp this truth, we must recall that the Hebrew word for man is "adam," and that "Adam" was appointed by God as king of creation in Genesis (2:19; 1:26-27; see also Ps 8:1-8). We are then in a position to realize that in an apocalyptic context which expects the New Creation, the reference to "one like a son of man" (authorized by God as his representative over creation) is a midrashic allusion to the "Son of Adam," or "New Adam," expected to reign over the New Creation.

In Daniel 7:13, the expression "son of man" is not yet a title; instead, it is a midrashic *allusion* to the exalted "Son of Adam" who has been authorized as the "New Adam." But by the time of 2 Esdras, The Similitudes of Enoch (1 Enoch 37-71), and the four Gospels, the midrashic *allusion* in Dan 7:13 has evolved into an eschatological *title*.

(The Son of Man title was the first regal honorific bestowed upon Jesus by the early church. However, the title was soon abandoned in churches where large numbers of *Gentile* converts were present. When translated into koine Greek, the title [ho huios tou anthrōpou] was identical with a common Greek expression which meant, "the man's son." To Greek-speaking Gentile converts, therefore, the title suggested nothing regal or majestic, and its midrashic meaning was difficult to recognize.)

(It was because the title Son of Man proved unsatisfactory in Greek that Paul avoided using it in his letters. He preferred to translate it into an intelligible equivalent and spoke of the Risen Jesus as the "second" or "last Adam" who has freed us from the curse of sin and death inflicted on us by the "first Adam" [1 Cor 15:21-22, 45-47; see also Rom 5:14-19].)

Although Mark only alludes to the title "Son of Man" in the account of Jesus' Baptism because of the account's complex compositional requirements, the title appears with increasing frequency as his Gospel unfolds; eventually the title is presented as the *key* that unlocks the mystery of Mark's Messianic Secret (8:31; 9:9-10; 9:31; 10:33-34; 14:62).

Mark and other teachers in the early church readily gave the title "Son of Man" to Jesus because they remembered his preference for the title, and it seemed to foreshadow his eschatological glory and authority. But the title also possessed highly valued *apologetic* significance. It was especially the *apologetic* value of the title that motivated Mark to use it, along with the titles "Servant" and "Beloved (Son)," to suggest the secret nature of Jesus' Messiahship.

Many devout Jews at the time of Jesus expected a *general* resurrection at the end of the age, but there is no evidence that any of them anticipated the resurrection of an *individual*. We can be certain that some of the Jews who heard the disciples witnessing to Jesus' Resurrection appearances protested that none of Israel's prophets or scribes had ever spoken of the Resurrection of an *individual*. (Even the important proof text about the *third day* found in Hos 6:2 ["and on the third day he will raise us up,"] and alluded to in the early creed quoted by Paul in 1 Cor 15:3-5 ["he was raised on the third day"] speaks of resurrection as a *collective* phenomenon.)

Teachers in the early church responded to the Jewish protest by appealing midrashically to the "one like a son of man" in Dan 7:13-14 who has been exalted *individually* into heavenly glory and is borne upon the clouds to the very throne of God. Upon his arrival, this august individual receives everlasting "dominion" (see Gen 1:26-27) and is authorized as God's designate in the New Creation.

The *individual* exaltation of the mysterious eschatological king in Dan 7:13-14 was viewed by Mark (and others before him) as a midrashic foreshadowing of the *individual* Resurrection of Jesus (Mk 9:9-10) which exalted Jesus into heavenly glory at the "right hand" of God (Ps 110:1; Mk 14:62; see also Acts 2:33). The fact that the eschatological king in Daniel is alluded to as the Son of *Adam* and not the Son of *David* would have been perceived by Mark as indicative of God's "secret" purpose.

Mark's apologetic desire to associate the *individual* exaltation of the "one like a son of man" with the *individual* Resurrection of Jesus led Mark to include in his Gospel the three solemn predictions made by Jesus on his final journey to Jerusalem. Jesus announces presciently that the "Son of Man" will be delivered into the hands of sinful men who will kill him, and he will rise after three days (Mk 8:31; 9:31; 10:33-34). These traditional sayings of Jesus were placed *by Mark* at appropriate intervals during Jesus' final journey to Jerusalem. Mark arranged the sayings in this manner to stress that Jesus foreknew he would die at Jerusalem and then be raised as the exalted "Son of Man."

The same apologetic purpose is expressed by Mark when he has Jesus command the disciples not to speak of the vision they have seen on the mountain of Transfiguration "until the Son of Man is risen from the dead" (Mk

9:9). Jesus' reference to the Son of Man's *Resurrection* in Mk 9:9 baffles the disciples and triggers their discussion about the Resurrection of an *individual* in 9:10. Clearly, the apologetic problem precipitated by the individual Resurrection of Jesus was still a live issue for Mark and his church.

From chapters 1 to 7, Mark intends us to understand that the only others besides Jesus who know about the Messianic Secret are the demons; they discover it when they are overwhelmed by Jesus' Messianic power. Jesus, however, exercising this same power, consistently binds the demons to silence about his Messiahship (1:25,34; 3:12), just as he later binds the disciples (8:30; 9:9). (The reason why the demons are bound to silence will be explained below in the answer to question 10 of Part Four).

In Mk 8:30-31, Jesus, while at Caesarea Phillipi, begins to reveal the Messianic Secret to his disciples in *private* (see also 9:31, 10:33-34) as preparation for what is to come. But Peter is shocked by the revelation and rebukes Jesus for imparting it (8:32). Jesus, in turn, castigates Peter for stubbornly rejecting the difficult teaching and asserts that Peter's view is not that of God but of men (8:33).

The bewildered unwillingness of Peter to accept God's revelation of the Messianic Secret *through Jesus* in chapter 8 is the reason why Mark follows with the Transfiguration account in chapter 9. Mark wants us to understand that *God himself* intervened on the "holy mountain" to rebuke Peter for preferring traditional Messianic expectations instead of accepting the superior, albeit unexpected, Messianic teaching of Jesus.

To that end, God himself speaks from the cloud that covers the "mountain of revelation" and discloses to Peter and the other two disciples the substance of the Messianic Secret which was revealed to Jesus at his Baptism. God concludes his revelation in 9:7 with the admonition that in the future Peter and the other disciples should "listen to" the difficult Messianic teaching of Jesus with faith and trust.

Mark probably intended God's admonition of Peter to also admonish any member of Mark's church who might still be troubled by Jewish (and even some Jewish Christian) objections to giving the title Messiah to Jesus. (Mark's mention of "Elijah with Moses" in 9:4 will be discussed below in the answer to question 4 of Part Four.)

The command which Jesus gives the disciples while coming down the mountain (9:9) indicates that Mark is using the Transfiguration story as an important step in the gradual disclosure of the Messianic Secret. Jesus binds the disciples to *silence* about the Secret revealed to them on the mountain until the time of his Resurrection. They will, of course, obey, but they do not truly understand the Secret; they are especially puzzled by the prediction of Jesus' *individual* Resurrection (9:10).

We saw above that the theological (not historical) comment in 9:10 about the inability of the disciples to comprehend the Resurrection of an *individual* had a basis in historical fact. We also saw that Mark considered this general lack of readiness to accept the Resurrection of an *individual* as part of God's hidden Messianic purpose. (The reason for the "hiddenness" of God's purpose will be explained below in the answer to question 10 of Part Four.)

Questions for Further Study

1. Why is Mark preoccupied with Messianic Secret theology throughout his Gospel?

2. What is "apologetics," and why should we expect to find "apologetic theology" in the Gospels?

3. What was the most urgent apologetic task facing the early church?

4. Why was John the Baptizer an important figure in Mark's Messianic Secret theology?

5. What were the reasons that convinced Mark and other teachers in the early church that they had to re-define the title Messiah?

6. For what *apologetic* reason was Mark predisposed to give the title "Son of Man" special prominence in his Messianic Secret theology?

7. What part did Mark intend the Transfiguration story to play in his Messianic Secret theology?

Part Four: Remaining Questions

INVARIABLY, WHEN PEOPLE LEARN about the nonliteral reading of the Transfiguration account advanced by modern biblical scholarship, a number of related questions occur. The most commonly asked of these questions will be listed and answered below. The reader is reminded that there are no easy answers to complex questions; rather, the answers will always cost us time, patience, and attention.

1. *Does the explanation of the Transfiguration account presented in this monograph undermine the historical credibility of the Gospels?*

If the explanation of the Transfiguration account presented herein is correctly understood, it does not undermine the historical credibility of the Gospels. On the contrary, it protects the Gospels from being dismissed as "mere" legend or myth by insuring that the genuine historical basis underlying them is distinguished from its "folk" interpretation.

Contemporary biblical scholarship reminds us that the Gospels were written almost two thousand years ago and do not contain the *scientific* kind of history which we are conditioned to expect. Instead, the Gospels contain the *legendary* history typical of essentially preliterate communities.

Legendary history remembers real persons and real events, but *interprets* them in accordance with the laws of the folk mentality. Because folk history is ordinarily passed on by word of mouth, it must dispense with all but essential memories and interpret those memories with the unwritten, but well understood, norms peculiar to oral cultures. Folk historians embellish and hyperbolize (i.e., artistically exaggerate) the historical memories most valued by their culture to insure that such memories will be understood and retained by simple preliterate communities.

For example, both the *heros* and the *enemies* of a preliterate community are "absolutized" by its folk historians: The heros of the group are idealized as *entirely* good; its enemies are villified as *totally* evil. Such hyperbolization is not meant to deceive, but to signify clearly which persons in history are the bearers of values prized by the group and which are not. The group's heros should be identified with and emulated. The villains in remembered history, on the other hand, should be rejected as bearers of that which harms or endangers the group.

We must remember that the ancient folk mentality has not yet learned to distinguish between ultimate causal power and many invisible natural forces. The folk mentality, therefore, naively explains these natural forces by attributing them to supernatural beings (God, angels, demons, spirits). It is true that such explanations are mythological and lead to naive conclusions. But it is also true that myth correctly recognizes that the law of causality is operating everywhere and must guide all attempts to explain phenomena whose causes cannot be seen.

Folk efforts to explain the unknown, therefore, are precritical attempts to understand the nature of invisible causal power. Such efforts should always be appreciated and never denigrated, even though they require advanced thinkers to make critical distinctions.

The folk mentality interprets events and assigns motives to persons involved in these events from the perspective of its own special needs and limited insights. When folk explanations employ legendary or mythological elements, such elements are always woven into the fabric of the event being interpreted as if they were original parts of that event. Such narrative embellishments help the oral historian to remember, and the audience to assimilate, the "meaning" being assigned to the past.

In circumstances where there is need to teach an urgent lesson, the folk historian does not hesitate to create an "event" which illustrates that lesson (as is the case with the Transfiguration story). Such an event, however, is never "pure" invention; it is constructed from remembered traits or happenings truly characteristic of the person or persons on whom the lesson is based.

We have already learned above that the story of Jesus' Transfiguration is not an "historical" event, but a "theological" event created to teach an important midrashic lesson about the prophetic authority of Jesus. We should now remind ourselves that the account is not "pure" invention.

The story is based on: (1) the memory that Jesus sometimes retired to private places with his disciples (Mk 6:32; 14:32); (2) the memory that Peter, James, and John were privileged witnesses to a private revelatory event during the public mission of Jesus (Mk 5:37); (3) the church's memory of the apostolic witnessing to Jesus' Resurrection appearances (1 Cor 15:1-8); (4) the church's *confirming* experience of God's own Spirit (i.e., the divine Self-communication as love) released by those appearances (Jn 20:22) *and* their proclamation (Acts 10:39-44; Gal 3:2); (5) the memory that Simon Peter was regarded by the early church as the premier Resurrection witness because he

was the first disciple to whom the Risen Jesus appeared
(1 Cor 15:5; Lk 24:34); (6) the church's inspired *insight*
that the Risen Jesus and the Gift of the Spirit mediated
through him are conclusive revelatory signs from God
that require Moses and the prophets to be understood as
preparatory (Rom 7:6).

Furthermore, the first Christians were heirs to a religious tradition which required the use of midrashic proof
texts in the solution of theological problems. Whenever
needed, midrashic allusions to the ancient Jewish
scriptures were incorporated into the remembered history
of Jesus along with the requisite features of legendary
history already mentioned. All of this means, of course,
that some parts of the Gospels (such as the Transfiguration story) must be read in a nonliteral fashion; we must
learn to separate the *original events* in the history of
Jesus from their later folk and midrashic *interpretations*.

The earlier mentioned theological crisis that called the
Transfiguration story into being was so serious that the
Christian teacher who created the story felt fully justified
in doing so. And Mark, as a folk historian who was
divinely inspired to commit the sacred history of Jesus to
writing, felt no hesitation in modifying the Transfiguration story to help teach the Messianic Secret theology
needed by his church. Both Mark and the creator of the
story had been conditioned by their culture to feel not
only justified, but even *obligated* to creatively interpret
the sacred history of Jesus in the service of God.

2. Why do modern biblical scholars think that the Transfiguration account existed prior to Mark's decision to include it in his Gospel?

A critical reading indicates that a number of non-
Markan traits occur in Mark's account of the Transfiguration. We have already observed that the story itself seems
strangely different, even surreal, compared to the other

events narrated in Mark's Gospel. In addition, Vincent Taylor reminds us (in his commentary on Mark) that Mark's customary language (e.g., euthus, "immediately") is noticeably lacking, and the mention of the "six days" in Mk 9:2 is the only chronological reference before the passion narrative begins in Mk 14:1.

Moreover, a number of unusual words are found only in the Transfiguration account, and one of them (exapina, "suddenly") occurs nowhere else in the New Testament. When we join all of this to the realization that the problem addressed by the account originated well before Mark's Gospel was written (c. 70 A.D.), we are led to conclude that Mark found the story ready at hand and decided to employ (and revise) it in the service of his theological agenda.

3. Why were Moses and Elijah chosen to respectively represent the law and the prophets in the Transfiguration account?

There is no evidence that Jewish tradition made this dual identification at the time of the apostolic church. Apparently, the creator of the Transfiguration account was the first to do so. It is not difficult to see why Moses was chosen to represent the law: Ancient Jewish tradition attributed all five books of the law to his hand. To think of the law was to think of Moses (Acts 15:21). But why Elijah?

The fiery Elijah was, by far, the most dramatic and memorable of the prophets who succeeded Moses in the work of guarding God's covenant with Israel. A survey of the cycle of Elijah stories in 1 and 2 Kings easily convinces one of this (1 Kgs 17-19, 21; 2 Kgs 1-2, 9:30-10:17).

We should remember not only that Moses was transformed with glory on Mount Sinai, but also that Elijah was assumed into heaven (2 Kgs 2:1-11) from which he was expected to return to fulfill a major eschatological role (Mal 4:5-6, which is Mal 3:23-24 in some versions). Also, both Moses and Elijah were renowned for their power to perform divine signs. All of these exalted attainments readily lent themselves to comparison with Jesus and might have been invoked by the ultraconservatives as entitlements to full equality with Jesus. (See Sir 45:2-4; 48:4-5.)

Furthermore, just as Moses received the law on the "mountain of revelation" while fasting forty days and nights (Ex 34:2,27-28), Elijah also fasted forty days and nights while returning to the mountain of God to escape the wrath of wicked queen Jezebel and to pray for strength and guidance (1 Kgs 19:1-8). Both men, therefore, were especially associated with the "mountain of revelation."

4. *Contrary to expectation, why does Mark place Elijah before Moses in 9:4?*

Given the preeminence of Moses in the religious life of Israel, we would expect Moses to be named before Elijah in Mk 9:4 just as he is in Mk 9:5. Furthermore, both Matthew (17:3) and Luke (9:30) reversed the atypical order they found in Mk 9:4 and consistently placed Moses before Elijah in their versions. How should we explain the unusual arrangement in Mark 9:4?

We should begin by remembering that the original purpose of the Transfiguration story was to demonstrate that the authority of Jesus has surpassed that of *Moses* and the law. We should also recall that when Moses and Elijah are mentioned again in 9:5 Moses *is* mentioned first, as one would expect. This suggests that in the original form of the story Moses was mentioned before Elijah in 9:4 and 9:5, and Mark altered the story for some theological reason.

Our conclusion is strengthened when we remember that Elijah is a figure of major importance in Mark's Messianic

Secret theology. For Mark, both the Messiah *and* Elijah, his precursor, are destined to come "secretly" and undergo tragic rejection and death. The Messiah comes secretly in the person of Jesus; Elijah comes secretly in the person of John the Baptizer. But why did Mark think that Elijah must be the precursor of the Messiah, and that Elijah's mission must be cryptic?

On the basis of Mal 4:5-6 (Mal 3:23-24 in some versions), Jewish tradition in Mark's day expected Elijah to return from the heavenly realm to which he had been miraculously transported (2 Kgs 2:1-3,9-12). It was widely believed that he would then preach to Israel and prepare her for the end of the age and the coming reign of God (Sir 48:9-10).

The Gospels indicate that Jewish critics contested Christian claims about Jesus by appealing to Elijah's expected return. These critics asserted that Jesus could not be the Messiah sent to inaugurate the reign of God because Elijah had *not yet come* to prepare Israel as prophesied (Mal 4:5-6). We hear an echo of this challenge in Mk 9:11, "Why do the scribes say that first Elijah must come?" Mark's response to the Jewish challenge was to assert that Elijah indeed had come, but *secretly* in the person of John the Baptizer (Mk 9:11-13). It followed for Mark that if the Messiah was destined to come in a secret and hidden way, then the Messiah's precursor, Elijah, also had to come in a secret and hidden way.

(The other three evangelists agreed that the Baptizer was an important prophet whose mission was continued and completed by Jesus. But they did not all agree that he should be identified as Elijah. Matthew concurred with Mark [3:1-4; 11:13-14]. Luke, however, preferred to say that John had come as a prophet *like* Elijah [1:16-17], while the Fourth Evangelist forthrightly *denied* that John was Elijah [1:21].)

After the introductory verse of Mark's Gospel, Mark begins preparing us in 1:2 for our encounter with John the Baptizer in 1:4-5. Mark does this by alluding midrashically to the promise of Elijah's return which he found *implied* in Mal 3:1 (because the return is explicitly stated in Mal 4:5). After John makes his appearance in 1:4-5, Mark proceeds to tell us in 1:6 that "John was clad in a garment of camel's hair, and had a leather garment around his waist." Mark calls attention to John's attire in order to liken him to Elijah the prophet (2 Kgs 1:8) and thereby suggest that John is the promised Elijah who has mysteriously come as precursor of Jesus.

The Baptizer appears again in Mk 6:14-29 as the central figure in a midrashic legend designed to liken his fate to that of Elijah, who also was persecuted by a wicked king and queen (1 Kgs 19:1-14). The purpose of this legend is, again, to remind us that John the Baptizer is Elijah who has come as promised by Mal 3:1 (and 4:5). It comes as no surprise, then, when Jesus, in response to the question of his disciples about Elijah in Mk 9:10, declares in 9:13 that "Elijah has come, and they did to him whatever they pleased, as it is written of him."

In Mk 9:11-12, just prior to the answer given by Jesus in 9:13, Mark (rather awkwardly) describes Jesus as going out of his way to suggest a "secret" connection between his own tragic fate and the fate of John-Elijah:

> And they asked him, "Why do the scribes say that first Elijah must come?" And he said to them, "Elijah does come first to restore all things; and how is it written of the Son of man, that he should suffer many things and be treated with contempt? But I tell you that Elijah has come, and they did to him whatever they pleased, as it is written of him."

Mark's labored strategizing indicates that the theme of Elijah's "secret" coming is an integral part of Mark's Messianic Secret theology. Mark also alludes to the "secret" connection between the missions of John and Jesus by relating in 11:30 the question by which Jesus challenged the chief priests to disclose their assessment of John: "Was the baptism of John from heaven or from men?"

We may reasonably infer, therefore, that when Mark decided to use the Transfiguration account in the service of his Messianic Secret theology, the mention of Elijah in the story reminded him of the objection still being raised by the Jews about Elijah. And even though the journey up the "high mountain" in 9:2 clearly signals the primacy of Moses in the account's original midrashic intent, Mark decided to give Elijah greater prominence than Moses in 9:4 because of the important role he assigned to Elijah in the unfolding drama of the Messianic Secret.

Mark actually had several reasons for placing Elijah first. To begin with, he wished to emphasize his conviction that Elijah, indeed, had come as promised. But in addition, he wished to set the stage for the important question in 9:11 about Elijah coming *first*. The question asked of Jesus by the disciples in 9:11 is an echo of the question currently being asked of Mark's church by the Jews. It gives Mark an opportunity to provide the answer he is convinced is correct: Elijah has already come "secretly" in the person of John the Baptizer.

By stressing the presence of "Elijah with Moses" on the mountain of Transfiguration, Mark also wished to underline the inability of the disciples to grasp the Messianic Secret before Easter. The impressive vision in which Elijah has just spoken with Jesus on the mountain should have enabled the disciples to recognize the "secret" connection between Elijah-John and Jesus. But the question the disciples ask about Elijah while coming down the mountain (9:11) highlights their failure to comprehend. The Secret revealed to them by Jesus at Caesarea Philippi (8:30-32) continues to elude them even though

part of it has just unfolded before their eyes in 9:4, and
was confirmed by God himself in 9:7.

Mark's repeated reminders of the inability of the disciples to understand the Messianic Secret are meant not
only to reinforce the secrecy theme, but also to achieve an
apologetic aim. It was common knowledge that the disciples had fled when Jesus was taken by force in the garden
(Mk 14:50). The Jews could contend (and doubtlessly did)
that even Jesus' closest followers did not think he possessed Messianic credentials; otherwise, they would not
have abandoned him ignominiously. Mark's response was
that *not even the disciples*, priviliged though they were,
could fathom God's Messianic Secret before God fully disclosed it by raising Jesus from the dead (Mk 9:10).

5. *Aside from placing Elijah before Moses in 9:4, did Mark make any other changes in the Transfiguration account?*

There are two other verses in the Markan Transfiguration story that definitely suggest Mark's editorial hand.
These verses are 9:6 and 9:7. After Peter's suggestion concerning the building of three tabernacles in 9:5, we find
the following characteristically *Markan* editorial comment
in 9:6:

> "For he did not know what to say,
>   (*ou gar ēdei ti apokrithē*)
> for they were exceedingly afraid."
>   (ekfoboi *gar* egenonto)
>   (italics added)

The language of this remark about the obtuseness of
Peter and the other two disciples is highly similar to that
found in 14:40 where Mark again comments on the spiritual blindness of the same three disciples in the garden of
Gethsemane:

> "for their eyes were very heavy,
> (ēsan *gar* autōn oi ophthalmoi katabarunomenoi)

and they did not know what to say to him."
(kai *ouk ēdeisan ti apokrithōsin* autō)
(italics added)

According to Mark, the tragic drama of the Messianic Secret (for which Jesus has tried to prepare the disciples) is beginning to unfold before their eyes. But Jesus' teaching about the Secret continues to elude them (even though God himself recently verified the Secret for them on the mountain). Since the editorial comments in Mk 9:6 and Mk 14:40 use similar language to relate the inability of "Peter, James, and John" to grasp the Messianic Secret, it is likely that both comments were penned by Mark.

When we move on to Mk 9:7, we find some of the same words which were spoken by God when he revealed the Messianic Secret to Jesus in Mk 1:11 ("You are my beloved Son") now being addressed to Peter, James, and John ("This is my beloved Son"). Mark repeated the words from 1:11 in 9:7 to indicate that the Secret revealed to Jesus at his Baptism is now being revealed to Peter and the other two disciples as divine confirmation of the Secret which Peter rejected "seven" days earlier at Caesarea Philippi (Mk 8:31).

In Mk 9:7, however, the revelation of the Secret is followed by the command, "listen to him." As we saw earlier, this command is a close paraphrase of the directive spoken by God through Moses in Deut 18:15, and was intended by the account's originator to point midrashically to Jesus as the New Moses.

We should note that there is no midrashic connection between the Christological title "beloved Son" (of God, Ps 2:7) and the revelatory authority of the "New Moses." The first title is Messianic and the second is prophetic in nature. Alerted by this recognition, we may justifiably suspect that the "pre-Markan" form of the words spoken from the cloud in 9:7 had somehow designated Jesus as the "prophet like" Moses from Deut 18:15 without using a

Christological title. Jesus, for example, is presented as "the prophet" (like Moses), without a Christological title, in the Eucharistic midrash in John 6:14.

Another reason why Mark is probably responsible for the word "beloved" (agapētos) in 9:7 is that this word is a key midrashic term in the "Suffering Servant" motif (Mk 10:45; 14:24,61a) which is part of Mark's Messianic Secret theology. The term occurs for the first time in the account of Jesus' Baptism (Mk 1:11). It was probably carried forward by Mark to the Transfiguration account in 9:7, and, finally, to the parable of the wicked husbandmen who plot to kill the landowner's "beloved son" in 12:6.

6. *Is it not probable that Mark's Transfiguration account was created to provide the church with a preview of Jesus' eschatological glory before his Second Coming?*

Such an interpretation is improbable because no convincing reason can be given for presenting the eschatological glory of Jesus *within* his earthly ministry rather than at its *conclusion*. (This does not deny that pointing to the eschatological or everlasting glory of Jesus is a *secondary* purpose of the account.) If Mark had wished to preview Jesus' expected *return* in glory, the logical place to have done so would have been at the *end* of his Gospel, at the time of, or shortly after, Jesus' Resurrection (which is precisely what Matthew and Luke did: Mt 28:16-20; Lk 24:50-53; Acts 1:6-11).

Furthermore, the midrashic emphasis placed on the *prophetic* or *teaching* authority of Jesus ("listen to him") in the account makes it unlikely that the story was meant to preview his coming as the eschatological *king* who will preside over the end time and the New Creation which follows.

7. *Why is there no midrashic comparison of the faces of Jesus and Moses in Mark's Transfiguration account, whereas their faces are* compared by Matthew and Luke?

It is true that both Matthew and Luke make explicit mention of Jesus' face and describe it as shining brightly (Mt 17:2) or altered (Lk 9:29) like that of Moses in Ex 34:29,35. Mark, by contrast, makes no midrashic allusion to Jesus' face.

We must remember that the creator of the account which Mark employed was preoccupied with polemical issues currently vexing his church. We saw earlier that this inspired teacher signified that Jesus was *entirely* transfigured with eschatological glory, whereas only the *face* of Moses had been transformed with merely *passing* glory. The moderating teacher wished to imply by this contrast that the authority of Jesus is complete and conclusive, whereas that of Moses was incomplete and preparatory. It was *contrary* to this teacher's purpose, therefore, to liken the face of Jesus to that of Moses.

By the time Matthew and Luke wrote their Gospels, the conflict over Mosaic observance had subsided, and moderation had largely prevailed. As a consequence, Matthew and Luke were no longer keenly concerned about the dispute that had determined the nuances of the original account. They both felt free to modify the midrashic logic of the original story by likening the face of Jesus to that of Moses.

Considering the later circumstances in which Matthew and Luke wrote, their decision to make that change was reasonable and almost inevitable. But at a deeper level, the subtle purpose of the account's originator is still discernable and explains the text we find in Mark. Mark probably honored the original account's refusal to mention the face of Jesus because Mark and his church were still aware of a need for the midrashic lesson intended by the original account.

8. Why does Luke say in 9:28 that Jesus was transfigured "after about eight days," instead of "after six days," as we read in 9:2 of Mark?

We observed earlier that Mk 9:2 is midrashically comparing Moses' revelatory encounter with God on Mount Sinai in Ex 24:15-16 to the encounter which Jesus and his disciples are about to undergo on the mountain of Transfiguration. Just as God spoke "after six days" to Moses of old from the cloud that covered Mount Sinai, so God is about to speak "after six days" to the disciples with Jesus, the New Moses, from the cloud that will cover the mountain of Transfiguration.

Luke preferred to begin his version of the Transfiguration story with a reference to "eight days" rather than "six days" because he wished to teach a different midrashic lesson, one based on the number "eight." The early church assigned theological meaning to the number eight for the following reasons:

At the time of Jesus, the majority of religiously concerned Jews in Palestine had embraced the eschatological hope taught by the Pharisees. Many of the Jews who had embraced this hope believed that when the Messiah came, he would preside over the end of history and usher in the New Creation promised by the prophets. Some of these Jews believed that a glorious Messianic reign on earth would come as a *preamble* to the New Creation. (More will be said below about this preamble in the answer to question 12.)

It is understandable, therefore, that some of the Jews responded to Christian claims about the Risen Jesus by objecting that he could not be the promised Messiah because the New Creation (or its temporal preamble) had not yet arrived. The Christian faith community replied by insisting that the New Creation has mysteriously *begun* with the Resurrection of Jesus. (They believed that the Resurrection of Jesus was the "beginning" of the end of the world.)

The Risen Jesus, they maintained, is God's guarantee that Everlasting Life in the New Creation will soon arrive in its eschatological *fulness* because it has already *begun* in Jesus. Jesus was seen with the eyes of faith as the foundation stone of the New Creation (Rom 9:32-33; see also Lk 2:13-14 which is a midrash on Job 38:4-7), and the gift of the Spirit mediated through Jesus was called God's "earnest" or "pledge given in advance" ("arrabōna," 2 Cor 1:22; 5:5).

In order to validate their conviction that the Risen Jesus is the *Beginning* of the New Creation, the earliest Christians searched the scriptures for midrashic proof texts. They were reminded by their reading of Genesis that the old creation had been called into being during a period of seven days, *beginning* with the first day of the week when God called "light" out of darkness (Gen 1:3-5).

They then concluded that God had raised Jesus as the "light" of the world on Easter Sunday, "the first day of the week," to signify that the New Creation has begun and is hastening toward its completion when the Cosmic Sabbath of eternal rest will begin. (See Heb 4:3-5,9-11 for an example of a New Testament midrash dealing with the eschatological Sabbath.)

Because of the apologetic importance of this New Creation theology in the faith life of the early church, all four Gospels announce that the empty tomb was discovered on "the first day of the week" at or near the time of *sunrise* (Mk 16:1; Mt 28:1; Lk 24:1; Jn 20:1; 21:4). This announcement is tantamount to proclaiming that the New Creation promised by God's prophets has begun with the Resurrection of Jesus. The early church included a midrashic allusion to the *first day* of creation (Gen 1:3-5) in her recital of the empty tomb story to remind Christians of the proof text needed to defend their faith in the disputed Messiahship of Jesus.

When the "first day" of the New Creation was added to the "seven" days of the old creation which it followed, it became the "eighth day." The early church's theological preoccupation with the "eighth day" left midrashic marks in several other places in the New Testament besides Luke's Transfiguration account.

The Fourth Gospel advisedly tells us that when the Risen Jesus appeared to his disciples for the second time, it was "eight days later" on the Sunday following Easter Sunday (20:26). For the Johannine church, the Lord's day had become the "eighth day" which begins the New Creation, and the "presence" of the Risen Lord in the midst of his assembled community was anticipated every "eight" days.

In addition, 1 Peter 3:20-21 speaks midrashically of the "eight" persons who were saved in Noah's ark as foreshadowing those who are now saved through Baptism and taken into the New Creation. This New Creation began with Jesus' Resurrection on the "eighth day." (From one perspective, Noah was likened to a second Adam who began the old creation anew. As such, he foreshadowed Jesus, the New Adam who has begun the New Creation. From another perspective, the "eight" persons in Noah's ark who survived the flood and began the old creation anew were viewed as a midrashic sign presaging that the New Creation would begin on the "eighth day.")

We can now see why Luke chose to begin his Transfiguration account with a reference to "eight days." He did so to alert us that the story which follows is a midrashic reflection on the Risen Jesus, who by fulfilling the divinely decreed portendings in the law of Moses and the prophets (Lk 9:31) delivered creation from bondage to corruption

(Acts 2:31-32) and inaugurated the New Creation on the "eighth day."

9. *Could not the Transfiguration story be a misplaced account of an appearance of the Risen Jesus to his disciples?*

Serious objections can be raised against reading the Transfiguration story in this manner. None of the accounts of the Resurrection appearances in the New Testament mentions the *glory* of Jesus or includes a *voice* from heaven, and they all place an appropriate *saying* on his lips. In the Transfiguration account, however, the opposite pertains: the glory of Jesus is pointedly *stressed* and there is *no* saying on his lips.

Also, in the Transfiguration account the word "ōphthē" (he appeared) is used with reference to Elijah and Moses, not Jesus. But in the Easter accounts it is always Jesus who is said to have "appeared" (1 Cor 15:5-8; Luke 24:34; Acts 9:17; 13:31; Heb 9:28).

On the other hand, the question we are addressing is not without a measure of correct insight. For although the Transfiguration story is not a misplaced account of a Resurrection appearance, it, nevertheless, bases its midrashic presentation of Jesus as New Moses on the presupposition that his Resurrection appearances have already taken place and are universally celebrated by the early church.

10. *Why did Mark think that God intended the true nature of Jesus' Messiahship to remain a secret until Easter?*

The answer to this important question had already been given by other teachers before Mark in the early church. These earlier teachers concluded that God intended his Messiah to remain hidden until the victory of the Resurrection so that the powers of darkness would not be able to comprehend and interfere with the Messiah's mission to free creation from sin and death.

This "secret" mission was destined to culminate in the permanent subjugation of Satan and all the other fallen angelic powers to the reign of God (Col 2:15; Eph 1:21; 4:8; 1 Pet 3:22). It is for this reason that Jesus is described by Mark as binding the demons to silence when they experience his irresistible power and recognize him as God's Messiah (1:25,34; 3:12). But how did creation become subject to the powers of darkness?

The early church believed that "Adam" had been created by God as the first King of creation (Gen 2:19; 1:26-28). But Satan wrested "dominion" from Adam through sin and brought death into the world (Jn 8:44). Satan then enthroned himself as the "ruler" of this world (Jn 14:30; 16:12) and, along with the principalities and powers who serve him (Eph 6:12; Mk 3:22), he now vies with God for "dominion" over the kingdom of creation (Lk 4:5-6; see Gen 1:26-27; Dan 7:6,12).

God, however, had foreseen the fall of Adam before creation began and had already determined to send a New Adam to free creation from Satan, sin, and death. Jesus was elected by God to be the New Adam-Messiah through whom God would secretly accomplish his saving purpose. From the Christian perspective, it is through the unexpected victory of Jesus' Resurrection that the powers of death and darkness have been defeated in principle. Their subjugation will be completed when Jesus returns in glory to restore the kingdom of God's creation to its original paradisiacal condition (1 Cor 15:24-25).

St. Paul had in mind this secretly achieved victory of Jesus, the "second Adam," (1 Cor 15:21-22,45-49) over the powers of darkness when he declared in 1 Cor 2:7-8:

> But we impart a *secret* and *hidden* wisdom of God, which God *decreed before the ages* for our glorification. None of *the rulers of this age*

understood this; for if they had, they would
not have crucified *the Lord of glory.*
(italics added)

11. *Did Mark create the Messianic Secret theology found in his Gospel, or did it exist beforehand?*

Some elements of Mark's Messianic Secret theology antedated his Gospel, but most of the elements were probably created by Mark to further clarify an already existing tradition.

The early church was initially unsure of whether she should confess the Risen Jesus as God's "Messiah." The first title used to honor the Risen Jesus was "Son of Man" (Acts 7:56). The title Messiah was not assigned to Jesus immediately for two reasons: (1) Judged by traditional expectations, the tragic history of Jesus seemed emphatically non-Messianic, and (2) Jesus himself was remembered as having reacted negatively to the title.

Only after a period of reflection did the church realize that, despite all objections, Jesus must be proclaimed as God's Messiah. The appearances of the Risen Jesus and the Gift of the Spirit mediated through him convinced the disciples that Jesus is God's definitive sign of salvation to Israel and the nations. And since the disciples were also convinced that the prophetic promises of a Davidic Messiah had to be fulfilled, and believed that Jesus was descended from King David, they concluded that Jesus must be awarded the title "Messiah." This meant, of course, that the title had to be redefined in a manner compatible with the tragic history of Jesus. Mark was a major contributor to that redefinition.

Ancient Israel's midrashic tradition had already suggested that there was something secret and hidden about God's saving design for Israel and the nations; such a view was implicit in the scribal teaching that all of God's future intentions were foreshadowed in the scriptures.

This postexilic conviction was intensified by apocalyptic theology which taught that the events of the "end time" were mysteriously adumbrated in the word of God (Dan 9:2,24-27; 12:4).

The early church decided, therefore, that God, in his wisdom, had concealed his saving purpose at work in Jesus to prevent the powers of darkness from interfering with its accomplishment. This way of explaining Jesus' unexpected rejection and death is already present in the teaching of Paul (1 Cor 2:6-13; Rom 16:25-26). Such an approach antedates Mark's Gospel and is probably being adapted by Mark to his own Messianic Secret theology in 1:25,34, and 3:12 where he describes Jesus as binding the demons to silence.

By creating his Messianic Secret theology and including it in his Gospel, Mark achieved three noteworthy results, one intended, the other two unintended: (1) He helped the early church clarify her understanding of the *spiritual* Messiahship of Jesus. (2) He enables us to understand how theological *method* was employed by a creative thinker in the early church. (3) He provides us with insight into the importance of *midrash* in the theological method of the early church.

12. *In reality, why did God send ancient Israel a Messiah so contrary to her historical expectations?*

By repeatedly revealing his presence and love to the prophets of ancient Israel, God encouraged the prophets to infer and teach that God intended to bless Israel in the *future* with definitive salvation. The prophets correctly understood that a "promise" of sublime blessing to come was implicit in their privileged experience of God's repeated Self-communication. Consequently, they assured Israel that when her response to God's gracious love became acceptable, God would bestow on her (and the nations) an ideal state of justice and fulfillment (Is 2:2-4; Mic 4:1-4).

God never intended that the promised "salvation" implicit in his revelatory Self-communications would be attained by military conquest (although a kind of struggle and conquest are involved). It was the prophets who assumed, in a culturally and historically conditioned fashion, that a final state of universal peace and justice could only be attained through *military* imposition of God's law on all the nations.

The prophets surmised, therefore, that since God had promised David an unending dynasty (2 Sam 7:11-15), God would surely raise up a Davidic Warrior-Messiah as the instrument through whom universal justice would be imposed on earth. By such means, the prophets concluded, God would restore his kingly reign over the kingdom of creation.

Initially, Israel thought the salvation God had promised her would come *within* history in the form of a Golden Age, i.e., a time of permanent peace, prosperity, and longevity, presided over by successive kings of David's dynasty. Only later (c. 165 B.C.) did she learn to hope for Everlasting Life in the New Creation. The New Creation would come after the conclusion of history and would restore the old creation to its original state.

The book of Daniel, in which Israel's new eschatological hope first appeared (c. 165 B.C.), did not suggest that either an heir of David or a military conquest would contribute to the arrival of the New Creation. Nor did it state that the king of the end time alluded to as the Son of Adam (Dan 7:13-14) would be a leader of earthly armies. (This is probably one of the reasons why Jesus preferred the title Son of Man to the title Messiah.)

Many of the Jews, however, did not abandon their traditional hope for a righteous and victorious Messiah from

David's line. After the crisis caused by the Syrian persecution had passed, they combined the traditional Messianic hope for the Golden Age with the new eschatological
hope introduced in the book of Daniel. This combined
hope is expressed in the "two stage" apocalypses which
appeared after the book of Daniel. It is also voiced in the
eschatological teaching of some of the rabbis preserved in
the Talmud.

By way of illustration, one of these apocalypses, 2 Esdras (also called 4 Ezra) teaches that God's Messiah will
come and win a decisive victory over all the nations; he
will then reign gloriously for 400 years. All who have
shared in his victory will enjoy miraculous prosperity and
longevity (7:28). This Messianic Golden Age will conclude
with the end of the world; it will be followed by the resurrection of the dead, the general judgment (7:31-35) and,
finally, the New Creation (7:75). In the Talmud, some of
the rabbis refer to these two related stages of expected
salvation as (1) "the days of the Messiah," and (2) "the
world to come."

Because of such combinations of traditional and eschatological hope, many of the Jews at the time of Jesus
believed the Messiah would come as a military leader who
would triumphantly establish the reign of God on earth as
a *preamble* to the New Creation. This blend of nationalis-
tic and eschatological hope is understandable when considered in the light of ancient Israel's history. However, it
fell woefully short of the saving purpose God had en-
visioned from the outset. God knew that what Israel and
all of humankind truly needed, whether they realized it
clearly or not, was a definitive sign of assurance from God
that humans can transcend "the terror of history" and arrive at ultimate meaning and fulfillment beyond present
tragedy and death.

The mathematical infinity of our self-transcending design gives us the ability to think about transcending

death and suggests that we may aspire to an immortal life of unending discovery and joy with God. Yet, our experience of guilt, coupled with our awareness that tragedy and nonbeing in some form can overwhelm us at any moment in life, makes us anxious and uncertain. We also know that when the pain and ambiguity of existence become intense, we can succumb to despair.

It follows that throughout our history we humans have asked urgent questions about the ultimate meaning of our existence: Can tragedy, suffering, and death finally be transcended? Is there an ultimate justice that finally rights all wrongs? Is our death a transition that leads to creative fulfillment, or is it everlasting exclusion from such fulfillment because of our past failures? Does God truly care about us and love us, or has he abandoned us in anger and disgust?

God knew that the best way to give us definitive assurance about the answers to our ultimate questions was through a human being who was truly one of us, i.e., a full participant in the problem of human existence. The Christian Message tells us that the human being God chose to work through was Jesus of Nazareth. God sent Jesus to us as his "guarantee" that we can transcend the terror of history and arrive at Everlasting Life and Joy.

In order to become God's Messianic sign of salvation for Israel and the nations, Jesus had to submit to the painful and ambiguous conditions of existence with faith and trust in God's goodness. He keenly experienced the tragedy, injustice, and cruelty of life, and the repugnance of premature and undeserved death. But Jesus did not allow these discouraging evils to overwhelm and defeat him with hate-filled bitterness or self-pity and despair. Rather, through the power of his faith in God's providential love and goodness, Jesus won the victory of the Resurrection and became the Messianic bringer of assurance from God that tragedy, injustice, and death can be transcended.

Through his Messiah-Son, Jesus, God has assured us that, despite its preliminary ambiguity, ours is truly a sublime destiny. We have also been shown "the Way" to live authentically in order to attain that destiny. God calls us to follow Jesus by living lives of faith, trust, and love which serves (Mk 8:34). If we do so, we also shall be able to defeat the "powers of darkness" (the personal, social, and physical evils in life which constitute the terror of history) and arrive at unending Life and Joy.

In his wisdom, God sent Israel and the nations the kind of Messiah-Savior that he knew they sorely needed. God foresaw that no one would grasp the true meaning of the Messianic salvation he had encouraged Israel to hope for until he raised Jesus from tragic and unjust death. The disciples began to understand God's true intention when the Risen Jesus began appearing and mediating the Gift of God's own love (i.e., the Holy Spirit; see Jn 20:22) in a reassuring and enabling new "Way" (Mk 10:52; Jn 14:5-6; Acts 9:2; 19:23; 22:4; 24:22). Therein lies the essential truth of the Messianic Secret discerned with faith by Mark and the early church. One who has fully grasped the implications of this Secret has attained the deepest wisdom and has experienced "the peace of God which surpasses all understanding."

Questions for Further Study

1. Why is it that the explanation of the Transfiguration account presented in this monograph does not undermine the basic historical credibility of the Gospels?

2. Why do we think that the Transfiguration account existed before Mark wrote his Gospel?

3. Why did the creator of the Transfiguration account use Moses to represent the law and Elijah to represent the prophets?

4. Why did Mark place Elijah before Moses the first time he mentioned them in the Transfiguration account?

5. Why is it that Matthew and Luke liken the face of Jesus to that of Moses in their versions of the Transfiguration account, whereas Mark, who wrote before them, does not?

6. Why does Luke prefer to begin his version of the Transfiguration account with a reference to "eight" days instead of "six" days?

7. Why did Mark and other teachers in the early church think that God wanted the Messiahship of Jesus to remain a secret until the time of his Resurrection?

8. Why did God decide to send Israel a Messiah who was contrary to her historically conditioned expectations?